I0528562

Oblivescence

Also by Kelly R. Samuels

Talking to Alice (Whittle Micro-Press)
To Marie Antoinette, from (Dancing Girl Press)
All the Time in the World (Kelsay Books)
Words Some of Us Rarely Use (Unsolicited Press)
Zeena/Zenobia Speaks (Finishing Line Press)

Oblivescence

poems

Kelly R. Samuels

Published in the United States of America by:

Red Sweater Press
P.O. Box 870414
Wasilla, AK 99687

www.redsweaterpress.com

ISBN 978-1-959525-99-8

Library of Congress Control Number: 2023916701

Cover design & interior illustrations: Kate Netwal

for my mother

Contents

Oblivescence

The Alpha Privative

Days and months are nonsense, non-
sensical. Only the year surfaces
and a season, recalled
from bare arms, canvas shoes.

Here are three words: *church*

velvet

        flag

Name them, again,
fifteen minutes from now.
After drawing the cube. After reciting
the days of the week backwards, and, too,
the word
                  river—

what flowed at the hill's base, muddy,
its banks crumbling.

Parts of this organ are going dark. Pulling away
from the skull, like a nut inside a shell—
      what we shook, listening for the soft rattle.

You shake your head, say: *I am losing*

my mind.

All the dates are nothing now. And where
the poppy is planted—a map is needed.   Here.

      This mark
on this page.

Misspoke

A ship, you say, is in the garden.
A ship. A sheep. A swallow.
Water. Land.   Air.

             You speak without realizing
you misspoke.

And why not water?

Nights of little sleep, the bed was a berth, the walls
a hull. The lawn an ocean. The hill a swell.

We stand by the back door so you can show me.

        It's old, with sails. And the white heather gives
way on either side.

In a Greenhouse, Early Spring

There are runnels
of greenish water we step over
as if larger streams, fretful
of our shoes. You mumble, claim
the hoses seem like that one snake
in the shed that one fall.

This is spring with snow
still in the northern corners and the ground
still too frozen to break.
                              But here—another season.

Rows of green and the flare
and the bloom of and the fringe.
You stand fingering a petal, softly saying, *soft*.
Asking, *What is it*
                                     called?
And if it will flourish
if taken now, from here, and placed
        there, even gently—
in the southern window for a time, the month of
flood warnings and streets rutted like the fields
you used to walk picking rock, tossing what was found
in the tractor's bed.

Over in another house we don't enter—hearty vegetables
and herbs. I talk of all the seedlings from all the seeds dropped
in cups on his porch, how they became
what could be devoured. But you want

the laborious delphinium, if only
for how different from, how useless
beyond beauty.

From the Greek: Horse and Sea Monster

We are inept
in our natural habitat—
some slower than others, making our way
in inches over hours. But

never mind. For we were not talking of
ourselves, but that named after. Forgive us.
See how we bend our necks in sublimation, the passive stance.
Do not chide so enthusiastically. Let

      us recall we were speaking of our eponym—
      that toffee-colored thing snuggled in
      that most important organ no matter what others say
      of the heart. And not thing, but rather things, for there are
      two, though we always speak of them in the singular. We

are only two conjoined for a short time, up through the grass.
Then her body slims while his swells
and then slims and then swells again until
he goes his way
and she goes hers
and all that remains must fend
for itself. Isn't it lovely while it lasts? Our

      namesake seems to have begun some sort of journey,
      though moored. Or not journey, but some sort
      of absence. You cannot recall what it was
      just then or where you were
      going just then and

the water is murky now. We try to proceed, hunched
and ridged and yet romanticized. See us, of silver or gold, hang
on the arm of a young girl you

      were once.
      Not pretty, this. Everywhere   scattered   pieces

of   paper as navigational tools.   And your hands
never resting long enough for us to recall
how beautiful.

The Dropping of (1)

Windows become
widows and you mourn
the loss. Say I cannot see clear
with cotton caught
in the screen, remnants
of winter on the glass.

And wasn't he a good man?

        The plate thrown against
the wall. Stomping down the hall.
All the silent days. Pout and grouse.

Spring cleaning meant the screens propped
against the west wall. Warm water and a rag

    while he waxed the car in the drive
and whined of birds.

You two birds, two of a kind.

Later, the purple finch flew headlong, lay stunned.

        Was gone
when we next looked.

Aperture

What you saw of me
        through it, I don't know.
You would insist upon stillness
        and smiling nicely and I would always ask
what that meant. And fidget
        and grimace, cross my eyes—sun
blinding.

Everything always looked far
        away, or farther—as if the gap
existed between us and not
        in the instrument, that variable space.
You'd say, *step closer*. Then: *too
        close*. Your hand gestural.

From Latin apertura, from apert—opened

        from aperire, to open.

You store the albums
        in the old record cabinet with the two
sliding doors. All the pages sticky, photos
        yellowing—the span of years
on the inside covers and on the backs
        of. And my name.

What you see now
        doesn't resonate. Seems
unfamiliar. Is this child you and when
        and whose garden behind, with the lupines
blooming like no tomorrow? You hold
        the picture closer, peer at—as if

trying to see your way clear
to the bottom.

Metathesis

Transposition: this here, then
there, quick as. ur, ru? Are you
there, were you ever? The two of you as girls
playing at anagrams, at palindromes. *Madam, please
refer me to...*

We talk on the phone while you take notes
and laugh, saying your skill at spelling
has gone, *has flown the coop.* Some days, you claim, *Someday,
I won't know who you are.* Even now, sometimes, you
just gesture, call me *you.*

This, in the car, with your grocery list in hand,
the word bananas always giving you trouble.
And we chant M-I-S-S-I-S-S-I-P-P-I as we cross
over that body of water and talk
of who you miss—all those long-dead people.
Dare we forget. There you are, dear. Read me

what I wrote.

What Summer Was

Cicadas and the racetrack meant summer. Waiting
for storms with attendant lightning—what you said
struck down that boy on the baseball field on the outskirts
of town—that town four blocks by four. A church here.
       Here.   Here.

The heat lightning the other night was distant
          and irregular. I stood on the second-floor landing
     to watch. Recalled how I once thought the flash safer

        than the jagged—that blinding tuning fork.

Nights of storms with either kind meant the races were canceled
and I slept sound.   Did not have to lie awake
to their feverish revolution
that seemed cousin to the cicadas in the trees
droning on, rising to a pitch.

     Summer was this: And this.
Washed-out light. An itch for the storm's blast
and clamor and spark.

It traveled only once down the line. Only made my ears ring
and you murmured, *Thanks, be.*

That boy, bored
with so few pop flies. Clouds massing.
Spectators claimed there'd be time.
There was a crack and flare. The smell—carried—something
you never forgot.

Climbing down the Inner Rope (1)

And what of that night you left me
in someone else's care and wondered after
if it was the best. And, yet, didn't return
to fetch me. Left me in the company
of strangers with unfamiliar ways
and quick hands. It was done
and so could be done again.
I had to, you would say. Why not
me? When I read the line in the novel
I've read three times, I stop
and consider words—the choice
of this one versus that.
It's not *shimmying* down. It's not *letting*
down or even *making your way*, but climbing—
what signifies ascent but isn't, here.
I'd sit quietly and try and recall
the color of the walls.
What smell.
What season
outside the window?
And all of this was difficult
and meant altering everything
I thought I knew.

What We Think of When the Character in the Novel Says There Should Be a Word for Memories Left Unremembered

The word is stubborn.
It does not want to be known.
Petulant and sullen, it hides
in the cellar stairwell
where it is dark
and the walls are moldy
in artistic ways.
We'd sometimes cheat
and peek while counting
to whatever number
we had decided on
and see what we shouldn't have
seen. But even this wouldn't work
today with this word
that, actually, left nearly three days
ago and doesn't yearn
to be found. It hunkers
with the best of them—
all those others that have felt
necessary all these years:
water, glove, blanket, bloom.
It resembles the memory
which you cannot speak
of, having gone into hiding
too. Somewhere behind
the armoire too heavy to ever
be moved. Somewhere
in the corner
that never gets swept.

Overwritten (1)

Fear would have to bring you here—
                to what had not been overwritten:

long nights with only *The Waltons* and a toddler
                whining in the corner.

Later, a slam and a shove with a rough hand.

Weren't they lovely—those years by the lake?
                The birches, the view. The one light left on.

Little Scraps

lift with a breeze

                                           from the door ajar

or open window—

A scattering of this
reminder, this list:

his birthday

                                           milk
                                           bread
                                           apple sauce, sweetened.

And we bend
at the knees to gather.   Recall attending mass.

And the lowering
and supplication.

You say, *I wrote it*

                              down, here.   In a width
                                            so narrow as to be
                                            a slip of

a remnant.

Anomia

So many objects become
things.

That thing, there.
You know,
that thing.

Sometimes a color is given
or a shape made with your hands.
Always frustration when I cannot
locate the word
for you. Or the place.

There.
Over there,
you know.

You say it's because your mind
is working faster than your mouth
or your mouth is going faster
than your mind. Can't keep up. Can't
keep pace, and you should
and I should.

And no matter, as you cross the room and pick it up and place it
in my hands.

(Narrative Identity, or the First Story as It's Told)

It's evolving—what with all that has been and has been reconstructed and what is currently and what is imagined when I think of tomorrow. How it will be warmer and my down coat might be left hanging as I drive to what was your house and continue sorting what now could be termed detritus. The dessert dishes never used. And the slacks still with tags. The glider with its coated runners and abandoned web. All those years you made me dust every Saturday morning, no matter what awaited—the scrap of chamois oily with furniture spray and resentment. Here, now, I try to see the good—that I'm here and the sun is streaming in through the bay window and, eventually, this will be in the past.

Recalling What Did Not Occur

What if I can remember
what color the leaves were
and how you said the one
tree was showing off, flagrant
in its alteration? We sat
beneath it, on the boulevard,
west of the church—you
in a folding chair, me
on the curb. There was
the snap of the seat
put in place, a settling.
A muddy sun but no
clouds portending
rain. Before the first float
appeared, you cracked
a hardboiled egg
in your delicate hands
and handed it to me
whole, as if sustenance
was necessary to enjoy
what cavorted and pranced
and played so near
us, going north to cross
where the marsh lay.
Nowhere does it say
that the parade ever
took that route in all
of its many years, nor
that I ever served as
its spectator again.
And, yet: how we stood
after, shaking the blanket
free of debris and stepping
in to meet the corners.
The distant beat of drums
and wayward horn.

To Know It, but Not Remember

You say:

I've told you this.
       Have I told you this?
               You know this.

The father gone mid-winter.
Scratch of wool and sobbing.

You say:

I know it, but don't remember.

Can only rely on: text on a page.
Unreliable others and their stories.

I know it's rained.
I know I signed my name.
I know something's missing

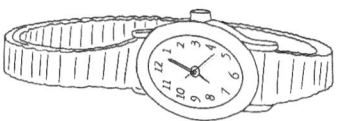

Oblivescence

This is the process, a series
of actions or steps taken in order
to...something. Natural or involuntary
or systematic, the last like those Saturdays
canning. What was first, and then
second, and so on. The enormous canner
on the stovetop with its rumbling
as you sorted and then peeled
and then pitted the peaches, their ripe
skins sheathes on the board, clinging
to the knife's edge. The juice ran down
your wrist, sticky and troublesome.
You coated the slices in preserve
before cramming them into the jars
lined on the table, lined on
the counter, before covering them
with the hot, sweet syrup and then
immersing them. The timer made
its harsh diligent way while I asked
of altitude and what part it played.
You spoke of Colorado and the one time
we were there and how your head felt
as if it would break open. And then,
the precarious lifting and waiting...
counting, for the pop, the final ah!

I would carry the jars down
into the basement for you
and stand them on the shelves
and much later remember
them when reading that poem
by the famous poet and think of
preparation and the wet, jewel-
gold tongues kept. This, this task
learned by you, not me, never me,
now lost. Even in this telling, not all.

Some semblance of narrative but
some necessary gestures absent, wiped
away: the rattle of lids and rings
and their tightening, for example.
Or, even, how I made my way
through that bounty.

In This Text

Weary is now wary.
The letter(s) gone, or unseen.
The optometrist's paddle over one eye and then only
these. Like that.

And as you write, each line
       indented. As if the space is not there
           or must be kept
               for something. Or as birds in flight.
What word specific to those?

You always loved cardinals, their radiance—bright
       bright. But never seen in flight as more than
           two. So, murmuration. Or a wedge—your missive
sent before we knew. And we would ask one another, *Why*
       does it look this way?
Take this away, here.

              And have that.

Scrawled on a scrap:
I am tired.
I am tied.

What Could Not Be Forgiven for Not Having Been Recalled

What is worry but wasted energy?

He took me to the courts while you wrung your hands
in a small room, waiting for news of who had always been
more like a mother—that woman bent to pick beans
in a stained apron in another state.

And there might be death
or just a long hospital stay.

I would work on my serve and my backhand, weak
for my weak wrists. All would be fine.

Thirty years later I ask you to forgive
and you ask me for what—not recalling anything
of that day but the call of loss and hurried packing.

There is nothing of my leaving before. Nothing
of my absence during. And if, on return, he scolded, if he shamed
out under the trellis with the spent morning glories then, well...

it was all so long ago.

What seemed immense, a wrong—not remembered
nor retained.

You'll tell the story.
I'll tell the story. What words
will be the same?

The room's walls were papered in green. No, gray.
And late in the day, the tree's leaves thrashed
in cast shadows.

We buried her in autumn.
We buried her in April.

There were roses.
There were lilies.

You asked why I looked as if I had been crying.

The Salt in the Pudding

You made pudding on the stove, stirring it slowly,
the spatula's edges curling slightly with the years.

Served it warm in dishes the color of the eyes
of the first boy I loved who didn't love me.

You favored vanilla and then suddenly
switched to chocolate and stuck with it.

Talked of change and the cocoa bean and how
with time you liked everything more bitter.

I ate it instant and cold, in containers I rinsed
and recycled, always feeling a little guilty.

The best was in the hospital's cafeteria
that winter when his bilirubin was too high.

I would make my way from the lit room
that fractured and cracked my head, and sit

to spoon it in—this sanctioned treat sweetening
the three days and three nights of fretting.

We always fretted, you and I. The wringing of hands,
even on days of joy—that bell, that song. What worry?

The slick curve and the bare tire, the man saying
the gray was showing and no long trip should be taken.

Salt would pock the smooth surface, alter all
that we adored. Be the luck that turned after being

thrown over the shoulder.

Alexithymia, Seventy-Seven-Year-Old Female w Temporal Atrophy

Snow melting and pooling
and threatening to breach the stoop
is of little consequence. As is the ice
from the door to the drive, the one path taken
resembling a glacier. *So*
be it and
        Let it be. So what—
falling and flood. Years ago
this happened: all the water. And still, you are
here.

Death of the nephew.
        Absence
of the frilled peony this imminent spring—no matter.

You'll stand near garden's edge, bend, root
in the wet muck of it
and shrug.

Cry me a river, you used to say, still say.

Climbing down the Inner Rope (2)

All he remembers is a blue cape.
And that the world was
saved—nothing
I ever did. Only
the one year, taken into
town to walk door-
to-door while the car sat
at the curb, time a-ticking.
Pictures confirm I wore a lei
and carried a ukulele
with mum strings.
And what of dogs?
How many?
Their names?
He says there was
Fudgy and Mutt
and he doesn't know
what happened
to either. Everything
was falling apart
then—that autumn.
Everything was too much
hassle and candy
was just temporary
and perilous, like
the wet, slick leaves
that had fallen.

Errand Paralysis, Seventy-Seven-Year-Old Female w Bitemporal Atrophy

To walk here and deliver
this asks too much today.
Today will be for delay, for
postponement. For saying
it will not matter to wait. Or prompt
anticipation for the arrival:
How we would listen
for the rattle of the box nailed
by the door or the sound
the truck made as it pulled away
from the curb, all the dogs barking
in that block.
          I will not
mail this today.

The envelope absent
of a stamp and the address
written in a shaky hand, the kind
of cursive not learned anymore.

Back when I was in college
you wrote me letters telling
of all you were doing.
All the *loves*
just form.
               So busy
you were, then.
With your early-morning calls
and the drive there and back
and your garden on the weekends—
the weeds and deadheading
and cataloging of all the lilies.

And then no letters
and now

one
that will wait
for another day.

Hand: Old English, of, Related to

The one says to the other it is like
one exclaiming they have no hands
and the other asking what hands are—
what functions and does and is so often
not thought of. Just there. Not missing
until damaged, until rendered useless,
even if only temporarily—the fingers
curling in on themselves, the palm less
meaty as weeks go by.

You could grip with the best
of them, digging in
when I didn't look both ways before
crossing. Could carry the platter out
onto the dining room table for its blessing
once a year. Tear the weeds from
the wet bed, roots and all.

We labeled objects around the house.
Left notes and other notes and more
notes, but your hands...you stretched
your arms out in front of you, waggled
your fingers, said *these, these?*

What Rises to the Surface

time

sat

murky

, suddenly

even the weather

.

it

sometimes

was

dark

Despite

day

on

day   .

And so,

a

kind of

boisterous

over. Often it was **unhappiness** and worry, but those are their own dramas.

When I was growing up she would assert, as borh she and my mother did, that I was told that I was a little woman in her stories, but all I remember is being angry at her.

What I understand of this now may be less than what it is that she may not have been happy much and that her moments passed, the she **dealt with** them for so people could experience it once in a year in those people's lives, just to get out in the moments it nearly nothing.

Maybe there, there are other memories for her. Once she dressed her in a sitting room, her hair un-brush, see. All her magic and needs. In the days and the evening, these were always at glass at the mossie everand.

Breakfast and second breakfast are so intimate hunted for **one** remembrance. We'd remove ourselves from the promise, we'd also remind us what I would run to see mother, because I feel as if we could ever go off and on.

There is a wonder in the lack of remembering period in a small presence. If my eyes without some shown at least, what able to eye, how dream later is me the words, rock, road, water, **green**

My mother's scent is half what I should be, my first thing. A specific scent for a thing that nLam some **shade**, but I fear **lost.**

Sometimes the memory is so much softer.

Do you like to go to sun and sometime she was held the water hopeless? Depends on what word I'm currently reading and who I might wonder with. One girl at the sea , but she's not much the
Yes

past decisions.

too, tired

regret.

Call it

landscape

And

here, my

mother.

always

Another

understanding

We do not
We   may not
entirely,
no.

once

waitress and sits us.

One month after that, I am sitting across from her, after having waited to hug for two salads and two bottles of water. She says, "I had three miscarriages before you." And I say, "That must have been awful." She asks, "Have I ever told you about when in Paris how I ended up homeless renting **a** room in a brothel?" And I say, "You did? Really?"

Six months later, after my stepfather too died, her tears stop enough that her memory loss diagnoses her with a mild diagnosis, the first stage of Alzheimer's.

When she asks to stop moving so I can toss a necklace ring-leap I hold her out, packing the groceries one while she modulates the **ground** after turning to hang her balance, her shoelaces.

Sundays I use our ground pick her up from church, **and then** take her over for dinner.

Most days we talk, her calling and then hanging up to me **.**

I send that to say our differences so natural, so natural, the dream we live, never stops, it never stops, so natural, never I remember to talk along or continue on a way and take my hat then to say, something along the way saying **Everything**

There **is** a long way. My mother and I are driving back from somewhere together gone, gone, and she starts to talk. She has something to mention, to say, something in her, mind being told, I watch her as she talks really, drive to keep across a road, as to drive, I keep to talk along in that minute, one her remembered. I love near the Mountains Wyoming border, the high-energy flux fogs... the... but the valley and... require to are nearly home .

Oriented by Three

Time was you knew the time and that late was never good. Would scold the dawdling girl who wondered why any kind of presence was needed when the sun shone so, and a light breeze ruffled.

Morning. Midday. Early evening. All the windowless rooms look the same. No shadow, no full-leaved tree or snow to show. This is the season of some sort of discontent. Chilly forearms, eyes watering. I drop you at the front door to find you wandering the lobby, asking *where, where* and a kind stranger, saying, *There she is, now.*

We've come around to who, whom. And we answer this, this the last to stick.

What Remains

Midsummer was when we first saw the dead bird
on the boulevard, near the corner. We said *no*
and *get away from that* to the dog
whose interest was greater than ours,
      though even on days we didn't walk that way, I found
myself thinking of it flat on its back, head turned, feet curled, like
the image of the finch posted online with an ode to—

      a blossom dropped near.

This was a robin. Had been a robin. Became less so
over days I've lost count of.
                A week or two
with the heat and drought, its fragile bones manifesting.

It was left to do what bodies do—

      what you refused years before, with the fawn.

In the evening, that evening, there had been two, you said.
No foe, though you grew beans and lettuce, squash
and day lilies, their buds like caviar—

          one year they were crowning at dusk.
   And in the morning, nothing

but stiff green stalks, nipped clean.

There had been two fawns and then one, the other flung
      into the ditch, long grass bent.

You said when you returned with gloves on, the fawn was dead
      and that you took it by the hind legs and slowly
and carefully dragged it up and out of the depression, along
the long drive, back to behind the garage, to the space between
structure and stone wall, slope to river.

And you began to dig until nothing could be seen
and you gave in to the understanding of another day's work.

Three days, you said, it took.
The clay dried quickly, hardened, needed chipping.
The shovel was small and your arms weak
and the grave must be deep
and clean in its symmetry.

You said you *worked like a man*, and wept—
as if what you buried had followed

       alongside, laid beside, came when you called.

I never saw the grave, then, being elsewhere, intent on other.
Never found the grave later, there being no marking. Just this.

One day, there was nothing left of the robin.
We passed by, as if nothing had ever been.

Tending the Body

And, so, the feet first. How
you never cared for polish. Would go

barefoot, but nothing showy or drawing
attention to what served.

Your feet small, like a child's
never browned in the sun for long.
No jewel on the toe.

Nor the hand, except a little one
on the left. Birthstone of clear water, of that month

of spring. No, not true. There was another of
obsidian, that protection and stimulation of prophesy.

Your fingers long and thin, the nails
plain and kept filed, the dust of your tending
dropped in your lap evenings after dinner.

Enough. Everyone talks
of hands. And eyes—these sections, these parts.

How you broke your nose
careening down the hill

that winter, the septum never
corrected. Your mother claimed
all would be fine.

Now, the bared nape, wisps covering
the cords. From the backseat, its landscape

as you craned out the window
that drive of hard rain.

This housing for the spine tapping into
the brain, the organ now shutting down, all
its spongy portions darkening.

And, so, how you look at me
with nothing of recognition, trying
to piece it all together. Make it whole.

(Narrative Identity, or the Second Story as It's Told)

And what of all the necklaces never worn? The one cut to look like a huge diamond with the word *love* carved into it. The weight of that around the neck. Knock-off pearls. The chain from your childhood turning green. All in boxes, some labeled. I recall you saying you never liked jewelry, much. Took your rings off at day's end and groused about dangly earrings. All now in a drawer that sticks. As an adolescent, I'd slow my step past the stores with the cases at the mall and you'd tell me to move it along. Nothing of use. Nor needed. Only the one band given, years later. And the one perfect disk with chips catching the light to mark something now forgotten.

My Mother as Anticlea, upon Forgetting

I will have traveled all this way only to have you forget

                      my name, to stand on something
like a threshold and question who I am
and what I have done with your daughter
who was sent for milk, never to return.

       Or, late. Well-late. Well into those later years of grieving.

Here's the trough to drink from to recall, shallow and bloody.

And, ah, now! a semblance of recollection.
And some of what has been until now unknown or unsaid.

Sugar, like the Delphinium

Toxic, but you ask
on return, *Where is
the sugar?* (That word not lost.)

The five-pound bag packed
hard, heavy as a brick. Dipped into.
For the coffee, the banana.
Even for the scoop
of cottage cheese, crystallized.

Time was you used to tut and wonder
if I was having some ice cream
with my chocolate. Would watch me
stirring Hershey's into the New York
vanilla and scold. Used to warn
of cavities—their blackened pits and ache out
and down into the jaw
and neck.

Now all the sweetness added.
They would say
she is
            sweet on him.
You are
sweet on it.

The Lesser Snow Goose

We are waiting in the waiting room—a space
labeled as grand, with windows that face west.

There's no sun on this day and there's been snow
early, so all is gray or grayish and filthy with leaves.

The birds appear in my window—five of them
coming toward, with no apparent sound.

The man sitting beside you speaks up, saying
they're snow geese making their way to where they go.

Three days later, I am out on a walk and look up
to see nine of them heading in a different direction.

There's sun on this day and their wings flash
with light and steady, sure motion.

They pass above me with no glass between, going
away, heard in that way they have of communication.

I say to no one in particular how kind of stunning
they are and how the word *goose* doesn't do them justice.

And I think of you and that other day and how you began
to shake when they called your name. And how you said

you weren't feeling that well, which was understatement—
the lesser phrase, the making light of, what we do to appear

effortless in our journey.

Image of Tau Tangles in the Brain

I first see a bobolink nest—not nestled
in pasture or meadow, but floating.

      Like your words seemed to do, the ends of
sentences trailing off as you searched for the right one.

I'm at sea here, you'd say—though you never liked
being out on it, only close, what we call adjacent.

                Waterfront property, with a path
leading right down to.

Bobolinks' numbers are declining because of where they lay
their eggs. Fewer fields, earlier and frequent harvesting.

From *long* and *claw* and *to devour*. These birds disappearing

      like the saltmarsh sparrow being drowned
          in its delicate, spotted shell.

The patches of oily black in the image aren't ovoidal, are too many
to contain life. And they've breached the tangles, found

      an opening, an inlet—a place or means of entry, or escape.

And so now there does seem more of the ocean, seaweed
          moving with the current.

Clumped, later, along the shore, just before
rotting, turning brown.

      Pebbles instead of eggs, worn down smooth—glossy
against the rough grass that catches.

What Is Realized as Missing

She shares she misses hearing trains on the island—
even the long pull that serves as warning.

The shore and its tides do. And all the sunsets
he takes pictures of and sends to others
where no sunset can be seen.

What was the name of that man
        who translated that book
we left out in the rain?, I heard a woman ask
a man in a bookstore now shuttered.

He couldn't recall.

They left through a door propped open
with a battered umbrella stand empty of umbrellas.

Wasn't it once there?, you asked me
in those final months—that vague pronoun, that unnamed
longed for.

Things My Mother Said to Me in Stage 5 Alzheimer's

You were still born. Meaning I had been
born by that time of which she speaks. Of her
in that city in northern Minnesota.
In *the old part* of the hospital—an X
penned on the window in the photo.

It was when spring felt real. As if
it would stick around for a while.
Down the hall, a different baby wailed, but not
for long. Was stilled. With maybe something
like comfort.

She used to say I took awhile
to cry that day. And from her perch
she worried. She asked,
  Is she? Will she?
How long until.

*You are the daughter of the man
I never should have married.* Meaning he
is regret, ergo...
But this is not the time
to feel sorry for myself.

And we make our way
to the hospital, to this room
that overlooks a courtyard where
raised beds hold dried grasses
covered in snow resembling ash.

I say, *Look at the flock of birds
swoop and land on the wall.* And she
can't focus, doesn't see.
This is not the time
for that.

The Dropping of (2)

Mourning becomes
morning, though not as early
as once was, even in the summer
with its racket of birds and insistent
light. It's a wonder

                   to have risen
and walked down the long hall
to the kitchen with its bright floor
and the window with the pine filling it.

You thought you heard him call for you
sometime in the night
               and then, later, dreamt
of your grandmother standing among
all her tulips now only black and white
in the one photo.
        Though you will recall
they were red with bent green leaves
             and petals that shed themselves
    too quickly.

Deep Sleep

You slept all the time those last few months.

I'd find you stretched out on the couch with your hands just so

      and you'd startle, asking where I'd come from, as if
I had come from afar—another planet, and why not?
     Such a strange girl from the get go.

Was it deep—this sleep?

Though by then, there were all the tangles, what is called tau.
     And we were treading in the deep end, being asked to
use a pencil to draw from one point to another.

Down to where the body's temperature cools
     and the brain does its cleansing—is where we should aim
for, they say.

And, so, the chill, dark room.
And the sound of waves, if we like, if they will soothe.

     And we'll wake, having said we never dreamt.

Climbing down the Inner Rope (3)

We were where there were
no hills—only flat fields
of corn and soybeans.
Only steeples drawing
the eye up, rarely.
And there was no father.
No check arriving
in the mail, or note
of apology.
One wonders
about the well water
and just how effective
the windbreaks were. How far
could sound carry?
You said you would wait
one more week
before circling towns
on a worn map.
It was a long day
before night came
to offer an excuse to lie
under the eaves
and be still.

Overwritten (2)

Despair would have to bring you here—
               to what had not been overwritten:

late afternoons over a stove and then at table
               with the evening news and a sullen teen.

Later, a hurled plate and a curse and a stomping.

Weren't they lovely—those years along the river?
               The pine, the garden. The one light left on.

Terminal Lucidity

Alstroemeria is the name of the flower
you loved, its dotted petals thin tongues
speaking of tenderness, briefly:
the one night he came to the diner
just before closing, sober, blue-tied,
his face a little fretful moon in the window.

         Here's a span of hours when the name
of every flower is given, and where planted, and when to cut back.

And where the two of you walked that night.
And what was said in what ways.

Will You Walk with Me?

And here we go, though we go
nowhere. Me on the couch, her
in the chair, her fingers working
at the blanket's edge.

She talks to no one. She talks
to someone. And then, me. Or
a version of, off to the left. As
if I am not there, to her right
rising when she seems in pain
to offer water and balm.

I was Honey Girl, once, before
this and that and the years we left
off speaking.

And now we walk in her mind
to where I cannot go. And maybe
there are daylilies and those birds
she could never remember
the name of, though loved.

It's just the drug. It's just
the passage, they say.

Incidentals

They're put here, for now. Set aside
for the duration:

one compact mirror
one ticket stub
a waxy tube of Toasted Rose

I said to her there was no need
to take her purse. I had everything
and though she wore her gloves on the drive, she left
them in my car. They weren't bagged
and stored—last name, first name—like
the ring she kept turning on her finger
later, and only briefly.

I learn the room is larger, now. That the body alone
goes to the morgue. And this man and this woman
sit and make calls asking for next of kin.
And, *No, I'm sorry, I am
not. No, I have no idea. You could try...*
All this takes well past thirty days.

What we're leaving behind
that requires retrieving: two keys.
A twenty. *The Collected Poems of...*
with notes in the margins.

There is no room anymore, as in
space, for these. And when, finally, the sister
is reached, she cannot come anyway—this area
sectioned off, kept from the healthy grieving.

Only later, outside, sun contradicting
our mood, are they bestowed
with orders to wait for seven days
to sort and sieve—the cufflinks beyond
comprehension.

It's a world
we have a hard time
recognizing.

In the bag they gave me
that early morning:

a pair of jeans
a shirt, pink
her ring
her glasses with their one
weakened bow.

Narrative Identity, or the Third Story as It's Told

Here is the dresser with the curved drawers housing the unhung cuckoo clock. The dresser with the scrawl on the back—from who and when and whose now. And what to do with? How my back used to fit into one of its curves. And the mirror cloudy, and so the image. This was the dresser that was used, then. And the pink chair with the brass nail heads that caught on anything soft. And instead of a desk, some heirloom that took up a whole wall and split at the seams over time, that was hauled away after being banged down a staircase that turned a little too sharply. She'd say, *Keep it. You might want it someday.* But, no, off it goes—strapped in a truck's bed, heading north.

Nepenthe

This cocktail
served at dusk—that favored
time.
So soothing—to remove
a particular sorrow. A tender
extraction. For

        what rises to the surface
so often troubles: night terrors prompting wandering
of the hall. *What if?*
        How could? I cannot
    see beyond
that other night
of despair, its need for keening—the rocking stance.
        All lamentation, so

why not
this warm dram?
Let it take
and leave

the rest.

Vesper Flowers

I cannot name one though I went to the nursery with her every April to wander the gravel rows and exclaim over the new bloom and tender frond. So benighted. I imagine this ignorance stems from the only garden I ever really knew—that large rectangle unfamiliar with shade that wasn't walked after dusk, or ever at dark. Scent was no use to her; the one sense she gravitated to: what could be seen. Earlier, in another place, sound and the needle set in the groove, but no matter that, now.

So, I spend some time learning what carries weight to those who rise to roam after nightfall, find themselves falling back on something resembling prayer. The vesper iris and the toxic vesper delphinium with its white eye. But more the lily and dianthus and jasmine, the wisteria that grows counter and not.

      The restive moths are still
catching what little light there is
                and later, the bat swoops low—
     startling.

Allostatic Load

That I kept working, standing in front
of the class, speaking of just how many years
Penelope had to make do, to make her way
to her room and weep and wail and weave
that requisite shroud, is a testament, I think.
Though no one said so, to me. No one ever
stopped me in the hall to ask how I really was.
I suppose because I kept at it, and well. Didn't let
on, fortitude something I was lectured on
by her for years. Her, dying and then dead
when all the papers needed grading.
Apathy and detachment, what they call mind fog,
came later. I'd sit and stare off and when asked, use
that old slang—spacing out. Out in space, floating—
everyone and everything seemingly far away.
It didn't feel like a load, but when I tried meditating
and was told to unfurrow my brow, unhinge my jaw,
relax the shoulders, I reconsidered. It had been heavy.
Still was, and what day is it? That question they asked
her, along with what animal, the animal sometimes
changing from month to month. Stress will kill us
some say. Do what you have to. I walk the one route
and another day, the other, and try and breathe in deep
and exhale through the mouth—what I couldn't do
then, all the surfaces slick with ice. I suppose some might
have guessed something—that I took the stairs
a little slower. Never a big smiler, but certainly not
smiling at all then, and not much now, though it'll be
a year soon. My ability has been reduced, I read,
from constant exposure to stress. And where to?
Outside my window, the maple's leaves are turning
too soon.

Mnemosyne

The garden as haven. Here, the peony
in pink,
          in white, and all the Baptisia. Their names common
on the map drawn and kept in the drawer
and brought out each spring to study.

This stem and leaf
known early on, in their sprouting from the ground, as
the first bars of a hymn hummed.   Way back, way back—
that kind of recollection.
                    The quick dart into the street
and the nine consecutive nights and that dance hall
with the folding chairs along the walls.   All the stiffness
of crinoline.

Muse, noun.   Muse, verb.
To sit by the window and look
out and see   beyond.
Nothing but
ancient
history.

Now the weed may be
the flower

or the flower
thought unwanted. The milk
of the lesser periwinkle just
white.   And later, the swelling and blister
and all the wondering why.

We have to laugh to not
weep. That mask conjoined
with the other. The tune played.

And lastly, baby's breath like stars
gathered, soft against cheek.

Notes

Metathesis is the transposition of sounds or letters in a word.

"Overwritten (1) & (2)": Ledoux, Phelps and others have learned that for an original memory—not one overwritten by misinformation—to be recalled, the pathways have to be retraced. Fear is one of the most effective emotions in this type of recollection.

Anomia is a condition where a person is unable to recall the names of objects.

Narrative identity is defined as "a person's internalized and evolving life story." It can blend both the reconstructed past and imagined future. Studies show that people who try and find redemption in their narrative identities and practice personal agency in their stories are happier.

Alexithymia is the inability to recognize or describe one's emotions.

The three "Climbing down the Inner Rope" poems use as their titles a phrase from Christa Wolf's novel *Medea*, which refers to the challenges of retrieving memories.

Oriented by three refers to a person being able to name the time, the place and themselves. Medical staff learn that a patient unable to name all three may have temporary or permanent problems with brain function.

Terminal lucidity is a phrase used to describe the hours, sometimes days, when a person with dementia suddenly can remember what they had previously forgotten. The person often dies shortly after.

Acknowledgments

Thank you to the editors and staff of the following journals for first publishing these pieces.

After the Pause: "Anomia," "In a Greenhouse, Early Spring," "Sugar, like the Delphinium," "To Know It, but Not Remember," "Alexithymia, Seventy-Seven-Year-Old Female w Temporal Atrophy" & "Errand Paralysis, Seventy-Seven-Year-Old Female w Bitemporal Atrophy"

Delmarva Review: "The Salt in the Pudding" & "The Lesser Snow Goose"

The Fourth River: "Narrative Identity, or the First Story as It's Told"

The Healing Muse: "In This Text"

The Lindenwood Review: "What Rises to the Surface"

Medmic: "Metathesis" & "Oriented by Three"

Mom Egg Review: "Things My Mother Said to Me in Stage 5 Alzheimer's"

Orange Blossom Review: "Misspoke"

The Pinch: "Mnemosyne"

Radar: "Climbing down the Inner Rope (1)"

The Rupture: "Oblivescence"

Sooth Swarm Journal: "The Alpha Privative"

Sweet Lit: "Deep Sleep" & "My Mother as Anticlea, upon Forgetting"

West Trestle Review: "The Dropping of (1)" & "Image of Tau Tangles in the Brain"

Gratitude to:

Caitlin Buxbaum, for her enthusiasm.

Allison Adair, Joan Kwon Glass, Romana Iorga, and Jane Newkirk, for their kind words.

Faye Ellis, for her love and good thoughts from miles away.

Kate, for her beautiful cover and interior drawings.

Alec, for his love and support.

Jeff, for all he did in those last years.

About the Author

Kelly R. Samuels is the author of the full-length collection *All the Time in the World* (Kelsay Books) and four chapbooks: *Talking to Alice*; *To Marie Antoinette, from*; *Words Some of Us Rarely Use;* and *Zeena/Zenobia Speaks*. She is a Pushcart Prize and Best of the Net nominee with work appearing in *The Massachusetts Review, Court Green, The Vassar Review,* and *RHINO*. She lives in the Upper Midwest.

www.ingramcontent.com/pod-product-compliance
Lightning Source LLC
Chambersburg PA
CBHW051231120626
46547CB00013B/1600